BARBARA BUSH
First Lady of Literacy

By June Behrens

CHILDRENS PRESS®
CHICAGO

Barbara Bush looks on as George Bush takes the oath of office as
President of the United States at the U.S. Capitol on January 20, 1989.

Dedication: To Terry Behrens

Library of Congress Cataloging-in-Publication Data

Behrens, June.
  Barbara Bush : first lady of literacy / by June Behrens.
    p.   cm. — (Picture story biographies)
  Summary: Presents the life of the woman who married
the forty-first president of the United States.
  ISBN 0-516-04275-0
  1. Bush, Barbara, 1925-   —Juvenile literature.
2. Bush, George, 1924-   —Juvenile literature.
3. Presidents—United States—Wives—Biography—
Juvenile literature. [1. Bush, Barbara, 1925-
2. Bush, George, 1924-   3. First ladies.]
I. Title. II. Series.
E883.B87B44   1990
973.928′092—dc20   90-2201
[B]   CIP
[920]   AC

PHOTO CREDITS

AP/Wide World Photos—Cover, 1, 3, 5, 6,
  17, 19, 22 (left), 23 (left), 24 (2 photos),
  26 (left and center), 27; © David Valdez,
  29 (right)

Courtesy of Ashley Hall—11, 12

The Bettmann Archive—8 (right)

Courtesy Permian Historical Society Archival
  Collection, The University of Texas of the
  Permian Basin, Odessa, Texas—15

Rye Country Day School—10

UPI/Bettmann Newsphotos—2, 4, 8 (left),
  13, 21, 22 (right), 23 (right), 26 (right),
  28, 31

The White House—© Carol T. Powers, 25;
  © David Valdez, 29 (left), 30; © Michael
  Sargent, 32

Official White House Photograph—7, 14, 16,
  18, 20

Barbara Bush holding three-year-old Dominic Bines during a visit to the Model Learning Center, a children's museum in Washington, D.C.

"I'm everybody's grandmother," smiled white-haired Barbara Bush. On January 20, 1989, she became more than America's favorite grandma. She stood beside George Bush as he took the oath of office as president of the United States. Barbara Bush became first lady of the land.

As first lady, Barbara Bush went to work. She wanted to share her lifelong interest in reading with

Barbara reads to children at Martha's Table, a Washington day-care center and soup kitchen.

those who could not read. She would reach out to children and adults all over America who needed help. Energetic first lady Barbara Bush made this her special project.

The White House is both home and workplace for Barbara and George Bush. In her lifetime, Barbara has lived and worked in many cities in the United States. Her first home was in Rye, New York.

Barbara Pierce, age seven

Pauline and Marvin Pierce named their third child Barbara. After her birth on June 8, 1925, in New York City, they brought her home to Rye.

For five years Barbara was the baby in the family. She adored her older sister Martha. Barbara remembers being afraid of her brother James, who was naughty and "did scary things."

Another son was born to the Pierce family in 1930. Barbara's new brother, Scott Pierce, was not well. Mrs. Pierce devoted much of her time to Scott. Barbara turned to her father for love and attention.

Barbara's father, Marvin Pierce (left), was related to President Franklin Pierce (right).

Marvin Pierce was a successful businessman from a wealthy family. He was related to Franklin Pierce, the 14th president of the United States. The family thought of Franklin Pierce as a great-great-great uncle.

Marvin Pierce was an athlete and a scholar. Barbara learned her love for sports from her father. He had a wonderful sense of humor and often took her side in family discussions.

Barbara's father was her hero and favorite parent.

The Pierce family of six lived in a three-story brick house with gardens and a pond. Barbara remembers it as a perfect place to grow up.

Many residents of the well-to-do community of Rye worked in Manhattan. Marvin Pierce commuted to his work as an executive in the McCall Publishing Company. Pauline Pierce looked after her family and did volunteer work for the community.

Life for the Pierce children centered on their neighborhood and school activities. Barbara was a bike rider. She also loved reading, especially dog stories. She and her friends enjoyed make-believe games, acting out parts from the stories they read. Barbara took tennis and swimming lessons and went to dancing school. She was called a tomboy when she climbed up to the treehouse her father had built for the boys.

Barbara was one of the tallest girls in her class at Milton School. Her height did not bother her, but she often remarked about being a little overweight. Barbara attended Rye Country Day School after Milton.

Barbara Bush's tenth-grade class at Rye Country Day School. Barbara is third from left in the second row from the bottom.

Tenth Grade Girls

Mrs. Pierce sent Barbara to Ashley Hall in Charleston, South Carolina, in her junior year. Her sister Martha had also attended this prep school for girls. At Ashley Hall, Barbara made many new friends and was active in dramatics and swimming.

At a Christmas dance in 1941, Barbara met George ("Poppy") Bush from Greenwich, Connecticut. Their parents were members of the

Barbara Bush was interviewed by the Ashley Hall *Newsletter* after George Bush was elected vice-president in 1980.

same country clubs, but these teenagers had never met. The next night they met again at another party. The Pierce family could see a romance in bloom.

Barbara went back to Ashley Hall after the Christmas holidays, and Poppy Bush returned to his school in Andover, Massachusetts. Even though the miles separated them, letters brought them together. When Poppy graduated in 1942, he

Barbara as Beatrice (far left) in a 1942 Ashley Hall production of Shakespeare's *Much Ado About Nothing.*

Ashley Hall to Do "Much Ado About Nothing" Tomorrow Night

took Barbara to his senior prom.

The United States had been at war since Dec. 7, 1941. After graduation, on his 18th birthday, George Bush joined the U.S. Navy. Barbara said goodbye and returned to complete her senior year at Ashley Hall. George went on to preflight training in North Carolina.

When Barbara graduated in 1943, she was invited to visit the Bush family at their summer home in Kennebunkport, Maine. George was

The Bush summer home in Kennebunkport, Maine, is at Walker Point.

Barbara and George Bush on their wedding day, January 6, 1945.

on leave from his flight training. Their friendship turned to a deeper understanding, and they became secretly engaged.

When George received his wings, he was the youngest pilot in the U.S. Navy. He was sent to the Pacific to fly torpedo bombers. Barbara entered Smith College in 1943 as a freshman.

On Christmas Eve of 1944, twenty-year-old George Bush returned home a war hero. The highlight of his reunion with the family was his marriage to nineteen-year-old Barbara Pierce on January 6, 1945. Barbara once said, "I married the first man I ever kissed."

After he left the service, George enrolled in Yale University. Barbara worked in the Yale Co-op. At the end of the first school year, George

and Barbara were new parents.
Young George Walker Bush was
born on July 6, 1946.

George graduated in 1948 with a
degree in economics, and the family
set out to seek their fortune in
Texas. Their first home was in
Odessa. They later moved to
Midland.

Odessa, Texas, in the early 1950s

George made his fortune in the oil business as the Bush family grew. Barbara was a busy young mother whose life centered on her family. By 1959 Barbara had given birth to six children—young George, Robin, John, Neil, Marvin, and Dorothy. Robin, her first daughter, tragically died of leukemia.

In those early years Barbara devoted her time to her children. Little League games, homework,

The Bush family: George, Jr.; George; and Barbara. Standing in front of Barbara are John, Neil, and Marvin, the youngest boy.

Sunday school, PTA meetings—
Barbara found herself in the middle
of her children's world. Often she
was both mother and father to the
five. The oil business kept George
traveling. He was not always home
to help settle arguments, play ball,
or bandage a knee. Barbara's
children remembered that their
mom made the rules for good
behavior. She played their games
and helped with their problems.

George Bush
waged a losing
campaign for
the U.S. Senate
in 1964.

17

The Bush family fortunes prospered, and Barbara and George became interested in public service. In 1966, George won a seat in the United States Congress. Barbara packed their bags and moved the family to Washington, D.C.

For the next thirteen years the Bush family gave their lives to public service. Barbara stood beside George, working in support of his

political career. The Washington
years brought Barbara into new
social circles. She made friends
easily, and the new friends became a
part of her family.

After four years in Congress,
George Bush was appointed
U.S. ambassador to the United
Nations. Then he served as chairman

Barbara Bush
leaving her New
York apartment
in 1971

George and
Barbara
bicycling in
Beijing, China

of the Republican National
Committee. In 1974, President
Gerald Ford appointed him chief of
the Liaison Office in the People's
Republic of China. In 1976, he
became director of the Central
Intelligence Agency (CIA).

Barbara moved her family many times. His work took George to 17 cities, including Beijing, China. They traveled from New York to Texas to Washington to China, and back to New York and Washington. Barbara moved into 29 different homes! Within the week after a move, Barbara had the family organized and settled.

A gathering of the wives of presidential hopefuls in 1979. Barbara Bush is second from left.

Left: Presidential candidate George Bush and family in 1980.
Right: The official residence of the vice-president on Observatory Hill in Washington, D.C.

In 1980, George Bush was Ronald Reagan's vice-presidential running mate. Barbara Bush became the second lady of the United States in 1981. She worked on community projects and as a volunteer. She hosted many social affairs in her home, taking an active part in as many as six events a week during her eight years as second lady. Barbara and George Bush traveled

around the world representing the United States.

Throughout these years, Barbara Bush had a very special interest in reading. She felt that many of society's ills were the result of people not being able to read. Barbara's son Neil had a reading problem. During his school years she helped him overcome that problem. She wanted to help others.

Vice-President and Mrs. George Bush wave goodbye to their hosts (left) after a five-day official visit to China in 1982. Second lady Barbara Bush (right) talks with children at a Reading Is Fundamental book distribution in 1981.

Barbara Bush looking at books (left) with children at The Friendly Place, a family center in East Harlem, New York City, and throwing out the first ball (right) at a baseball game in Shea Stadium.

Barbara gave her time and energy to literacy projects. (Literacy is the ability to read and write.) She learned that many children and adults in the United States cannot read. Barbara joined organizations to help these people.

In 1988, George Bush was elected president of the United States and

President and Mrs. Bush with their children and grandchildren at Camp David in Maryland

in 1989 Barbara Bush became first lady. This mother of five, with eleven grandchildren, set a new role model for America's first ladies. The people of America knew Barbara Bush. She had already won their respect. It did not take long for her to become the most popular first lady in recent years.

Barbara visiting schools and Head Start programs (left and center) and helping prepare sandwiches for the homeless at Martha's Table in Washington

Barbara Bush made literacy and the importance of reading her special project as first lady. She said, "Our young people need to know that reading is a joy as well as the most essential of skills, and that libraries are inviting, accessible places dedicated to the joy of reading."

Barbara Bush became the chairperson for the 1989 Year of the Young Reader. She worked on her special project in many ways. She sponsored literacy volunteers, served on committees, and became chairperson for many reading organizations. She called for community support of schools. Barbara Bush made many visits around the United States to support literacy and reading projects.

Barbara Bush takes part in the Pledge of Allegiance during a visit to the W.W. Ashurst Elementary School in Quantico, Virginia.

The Barbara Bush Foundation for Family Literacy provides funding for special programs. A major goal is to "help every family in the nation understand that the home is the child's first school, that the parent is the child's first teacher, and that reading is the child's first subject."

Barbara Bush has received many honors. She has been awarded the honorary degree of Doctor of Humane Letters from three colleges.

Barbara Bush tends her flower garden at Kennebunkport. The family dog, Millie, had puppies in 1989.

Barbara Bush is a first lady with many interests. She has always enjoyed sports, and takes an active part in family games. She spends hours in her flower garden. Needlepoint is a quiet activity that holds her interest. And Mrs. Bush loves dogs. Millie, the family dog, is often the center of her attention. But for Barbara Bush, the greatest joy is being with her family.

Barbara's grown children tell of a childhood home filled with love. They remember an energetic mother who liked to tease and had a ready wit. This mom was organized. She had to be, with five children to manage. She believed in order, from clean rooms to a neat appearance. This was a mom who could hit a

Lunchtime at Kennebunkport. Barbara cooks a simple meal for the family.